D1518637

English in 10 Minutes a Day (For High-Beginners):

Learn Hundreds of English Words, Phrases, Expressions & More

Jackie Bolen

www.eslspeaking.org

Table of Contents

About the Author: Jackie Bolen

I taught English in South Korea for 10 years to every level and type of student. I've taught every age from kindergarten kids to adults. These days, I'm teaching in Vancouver, Canada.

I hold a Master of Arts in Psychology and the CELTA and DELTA teacher certification programs. You can find me here:

Pinterest: www.pinterest.com/eslspeaking

YouTube: www.youtube.com/@JackieBolen

Email: jb.business.online@gmail.com

Website: www.eslspeaking.org

Introduction

Welcome to this book designed to help you expand your English skills. My goal is to help you speak, write, read, and listen more fluently in just 10 minutes a day.

Let's face it, English can be difficult to master, even for the best students. In this book, you'll find dialogues, expressions, phrases, and other vocabulary that are ideal for high-beginners.

The best way to learn new vocabulary is in context. Be sure to do the following:

– Review frequently.

– Try to use some of the phrases and expressions in real life.

– Don't be nervous about making mistakes. That's how you'll get better at English!

– Consider studying with a friend so you can help each other stay motivated.

– Use a notebook and write down new words, expressions, etc. that you run across. Review frequently so that they stay fresh in your mind.

– Be sure to answer the questions at the end of each dialogue. I recommend trying to do this from memory. No peeking!

– I recommend doing one dialogue a day. This will be more beneficial than finishing the entire book in a week or two.

Vocabulary #1

A Couple of minutes
Meaning: Two minutes.

Examples:

Please wait. I'll be ready in *a couple of minutes*.

I need *a couple of minutes* to finish this.

You only have *a couple of minutes* before we need to leave. Are you ready?

After dinner
Meaning: When the evening meal is finished.

Examples:

Let's go for a walk *after dinner*.

Please do your homework *after dinner*.

After dinner, let's clean up the kitchen together.

Again
Meaning: Another time.

Examples:

Please do this *again.* It's not good enough.

Can we see that movie *again*? It's so good!

As soon as possible
Meaning: Quickly; at the first possible opportunity.

Examples:

This needs to get done *as soon as possible*.

Let's fix that toilet *as soon as possible*. It's leaking.

He'll need to get surgery *as soon as possible*. It's serious.

A waste of time
Meaning: Doing something that is not helpful or doesn't produce results.

Examples:

This homework is *a waste of time.* Why do I have to do it?

Cleaning my room is *a waste of time*! It'll be messy again tomorrow.

Most things I do at work are *a waste of time*.

Bad luck
Meaning: Describes a series of unfortunate circumstances.

Examples:

Ted always seems to have *bad luck.*

Oh no! I can't believe that happened. It's such *bad luck.*

I only have *bad luck*, never good luck.

Bad news
Meaning: Not good news.

Examples:

Bad news. You have to work late tonight. We need to finish this.

I got some *bad news* about my grandpa today. He's in the hospital.

Bad news! The deal fell through.

Practice

a couple of minutes, a waste of time, bad news, again, after dinner, as soon as possible, bad luck

1. Please let me know your answer _____.

2. I have some _____ for you. Please sit down.

3. This homework is _____.

4. _____, let's go for a walk.

5. It'll only take _____ to finish it.

6. Please do it _____. I can't read what you wrote.

Answers

1. as soon as possible

2. bad news

3. a waste of time.

4. After dinner

5. a couple of minutes

6. again

Dialogue #1: Turn Up the Music

Tom can't hear well and wants to turn up the music.

Tom: Do you mind if I turn up the music? I love this song. I can't hear that well in my old age!

Jenny: No, go ahead. It's fine with me. It is a bit quiet for me as well.

Tom: I'd love to turn the heat up a bit too. It's freezing in here.

Jenny: Sure, I can do that. It'll take a while to heat up though. Do you want to borrow a sweater or a blanket?

Tom: I'd love that blanket, please. I don't know what's wrong with me. I'm always cold these days.

Jenny: Are you feeling okay? Maybe something is going on?

Tom: I don't know. I just had a check-up at the doctor and everything was good.

Check your Understanding

1. What are Tom's problems?

2. Is Tom sick?

3. Does Tom borrow a sweater from Jenny?

Answers

1. He can't hear the music well and he's also cold.

2. No, he isn't.

3. No, he doesn't. He borrows a blanket.

Story #1: The Hare the Tortoise

Once upon a time, there was a **tortoise** and a **hare** in a big forest. The tortoise was slow, but he always kept moving, and the hare was very fast but a little lazy. One sunny day, the hare said, "Let's have a race, Mr. Tortoise! I'm sure I'll win."

The tortoise agreed, and all the animals gathered to watch. The race started, and the hare quickly raced ahead. Feeling confident, the hare decided to take a nap under a tree.

While the hare was sleeping, the tortoise kept going, step by step. Slowly but surely, he got closer to the finish line. When the hare woke up and saw the tortoise near the finish line, he raced as fast as he could, but it was too late. The tortoise had already won the race.

The animals **cheered** for the tortoise, teaching everyone that being slow and steady can sometimes be better than being fast and **lazy**.

The Moral

The lesson of "The Tortoise and the Hare" is to keep going and not to be too confident. The story shows that even if you're not the fastest, if you work hard and don't give up, you can still win in the end. So, it's like saying, "Slow and steady wins the race."

Vocabulary

tortoise: A kind of turtle.

hare: A kind of rabbit.

cheered: Shouted encouragement and support.

lazy: Not a hard worker.

Comprehension Questions

1. Why did the hare decide to take a nap during the race?

2. What was the tortoise's strategy during the race?

3. What happened when the hare woke up from his nap?

4. How did the other animals in the forest react to the outcome of the race?

5. What is the moral of the story?

Answers

1. The hare decided to take a nap because he thought he could win easily.

2. The tortoise's strategy was to keep moving slowly and steadily.

3. The hare woke up to find the tortoise nearing the finish line, and he rushed to catch up, but it was too late.

4. The other animals cheered for the tortoise.

5. The moral of the story is that slow and steady wins the race.

Expressions #1

I gotta run. (Very informal)

Okay, talk to you later.

Let's chat later, okay?

Sure, sounds good.

Yeah, let's catch up again next week.

I need to get back to work.

I do too!

Can we talk more about this tomorrow?

Sure, no problem.

Of course.

See you later.

Okay.

I'm off now.

Okay, catch you later.

I gotta get going.

Sure, I'll see you later.

Dialogue #1:

Tom: Hey Jenny, I'm afraid that I gotta run. Can we talk more about this tomorrow?

Jenny: Sure, sounds good. I need to get back to work too.

Tom: Okay, chat later my friend.

Jenny: Sure.

Dialogue #2:

Tim: So, I think I need to get back to work.

Carrie: Oh, me too! That newsletter isn't going to write itself.

Tim: I know, right? Same with my report.

Carrie: We don't get paid the big bucks for nothing!

Phrasal Verbs #1: Break Up

Keith is talking to his friend about breaking up with his boyfriend.

Carrie: Did you **break up** with Chris yet?

Keith: I was hoping you wouldn't ask me that question! I can't **go through with** it. I'm worried that he's going to be **pissed off** at me.

Carrie: You can **let him off** easily though, right? Be super kind. I know that you don't like **hanging around** with him.

Keith: It's true, yes. I need to **shake things up** and finally end it. Let me go do it right now before I **talk myself out of** it.

Vocabulary

break up: End a romantic relationship.

go through with: Do something that you have planned in advance.

pissed off: Be angry at someone or about something.

let him off: Release.

hanging around: Spending time with.

shake things up: Make a change.

talk myself out of: Convince yourself not to do something.

Practice

1. I think you should _____ with Tony. He's not a good guy!

2. Jay is _____ because I made him clean his room.

3. I have to not _____ asking women out. I just get so nervous

4. Sid and Jen are _____ together a lot these days. Maybe they'll start dating?

5. I'm not sure I can _____ the tattoo. It seems so painful.

6. We need to _____ a bit. Maybe we need to fire one of the low-performers?

7. I'm not sure you should _____ so easily. He needs some punishment for what he did. You don't always need to be the good guy.

Answers

1. break up

2. pissed off

3. talk myself out of

4. hanging around

5. go through with

6. shake things up

7. let him off

Time Expressions #1: Wasting Time

Kim and Sally about talking about summer vacation plans.

Kim: What are you up to **this summer vacation**?

Sally: Oh, every summer, we head to our cabin at Lake Minnewanka.

Kim: Wow! I didn't know you had a cabin there.

Sally: Yeah, we bought it **5 years ago** and **since then**, have spent **as much time as possible** there. It's the perfect place for **wasting time**, doing almost nothing.

Kim: Well, you need to **make time** to relax, right?

Sally: Definitely.

Kim: When are you headed out?

Sally: Actually, the **day after tomorrow**. I need to get home and pack **tonight.**

Kim: Okay, have an awesome trip!

Vocabulary

this summer vacation: Usually refers to time off that people have from school or work during July or August (in North America).

5 years ago: Now is 2021. 5 years ago = 2016.

since then: After a certain point in the past.

as much time as possible: The maximum amount, taking into account restrictions like school or work.

wasting time: Not doing much.

make time: Spend time doing important things.

day after tomorrow: In 2 days. For example, today is Monday. Day after tomorrow = Wednesday.

tonight: The current day, evening hours.

Practice

1. Are you busy _____? Let's go on a bike ride.

2. _____, I've been doing way better.

3. I'm going to Japan the _____.

4. I always _____ for the people that are important in my life.

5. I graduated from high school _____.

6. _____ is what summer vacation is all about!

7. _____, I'd love to finally read those books that have been sitting on my nightstand for months!

8. I try to spend _____ outside. It's great for mental health.

Answers

1. tonight

2. since then

3. day after tomorrow

4. make time

5. 5 years ago

6. wasting time

7. this summer vacation

8. as much time as possible

Vocabulary #2

Best of luck

Meaning: A wish that someone will succeed at what they're doing.

Examples:

Best of luck with your move. I hope that it goes well.

Hey, *best of luck* with your wedding! I'm sorry that I can't make it.

Best of luck with your new job. You're going to do well.

Big plans

Meaning: Plans that are not usual (in a good way).

Examples:

Do you have any *big plans* for the weekend?

I have some *big plans* for summer. I'm going to Italy.

I wish I had some *big plans*. I'll probably just stay home this weekend.

Boss

Meaning: The person in charge (at the top) at work.

Examples:

My *boss* is terrible.

I want to be the *boss* one day.

The most important thing at work to me is having a good *boss*.

Break Down

Meaning: Describes something that stops working (a car, for example) or when a person gets upset. Broke down = past.

Examples:

My car is going to *break down* soon. It's making a terrible noise.

He *broke down* after hearing that his father died.

My computer *broke down* at the worst time. I had to finish a report.

Business trip

Meaning: Travel for work.

Examples:

I have a *business trip* next week.

You go on so many *business trips.*

I hate *business trips*. I don't like being away from home.

Calm down

Meaning: Relax.

Examples:

Hey, *calm down*. It's not a big deal.

It's hard for me to *calm down* and go to sleep right after work.

You need to *calm down*. Stop yelling.

Car accident

Meaning: When a car hits an object, another car, person, etc.

Examples:

I got into a *car accident* last year.

Have you ever been in a *car accident*?

Practice

big plans, calm down, best of luck, car accident, broke down, business trip

1. Do you have any _____ for the weekend?

2. My car _____ last might and my boyfriend had to come help me.

3. Hey, _____. This isn't that important.

4. I'm going on a _____ to Norway next month.

5. _____ on your exam! I hope it goes well.

Answers

1. big plans

2. broke down

3. calm down

4. business trip

5. best of luck

Dialogue #2: The Sleepover

Tim is asking his Mom if he can have a sleepover at his friend's house.

Tim: Hey Mom, can I stay at Tony's house tonight? He just invited me.

Carrie: Are his parents going to be home?

Tim: Of course they are!

Carrie: It is a school night though, right? I don't think that's a good idea.

Tim: No, remember it's a holiday tomorrow. It's a day off because of parent-teacher interviews.

Carrie: Oh, that's right. I forgot about that. Sure, you can. I'll give his parents a quick call first though. What time will you go over?

Tim: He said to come over for dinner so maybe around 6:00.

Carrie: Okay. I can give you a ride.

Check your Understanding

1. Does Tim have school tomorrow?

2. Is Tim allowed to go to the sleepover?

3. When is Tim going over to his friend's house?

Answers

1. No, he doesn't.

2. Yes, he is but his Mom will call Tony's parents first.

3. He will go over at 6:00.

Story #2: The Bear and the Bee

Once upon a time, in a sunny meadow, there was a big bear and a busy bee. The bear was strong, and the bee loved making honey. One day, the bear asked the bee, "Can I have some honey, please?"

The bee had an idea and said, "Sure, but let's have a **contest**. We'll see who can gather the most flowers. The winner gets the honey!" So, they both went to collect flowers. The bee flew quickly from flower to flower, and the bear picked flowers with his big paws.

When they counted the flowers, the bee had more. The bee said, "See, hard work pays off!" The bear smiled and agreed. They shared the honey and became friends, learning that working hard is important.

The story teaches us that doing our best brings the sweetest **rewards.**

The Moral

The moral of the story is that working hard is important, and it can bring good things. Even if someone is big and strong, someone smaller who works really hard can achieve success too. In the story, the bee showed the bear that effort matters more than size.

Vocabulary

contest: An event where people compete with each other.

rewards: Something given to recognize an achievement.

Comprehension Questions

1. Why did the bear approach the bee in the first place?

2. What challenge did the bee propose to the bear?

3. Who won the flower-gathering challenge, and how did they determine the winner?

4. What did the bear learn from the bee's challenge?

5. How did the bear and the bee's relationship change after the challenge?

Answers

1. The bear approached the bee because he wanted to taste the bee's honey.

2. The bee challenged the bear to see who could gather the most flowers.

3. The bee won. They counted the flowers to determine the winner.

4. The bear learned that hard work and effort are more important than size and strength.

5. The bear and the bee became friends.

Expressions #2

Sorry to have kept you waiting.

Oh, it's fine. You're not that late.

It's okay. Don't worry about it.

Sorry I'm late.

Please don't let it happen again. (To a student or child.)

No problem.

I'm sorry for missing your message.

It's okay. I'm happy that I got a hold of you.

Excuse me, please/Pardon me.

Sure, no problem.

Sorry for bumping into you.

No worries.

My apologies for _____ (many answers possible).

It's okay.

My bad. (Very informal)

No problem.

Dialogue #1:

Tom: Oh hey Jenny. Sorry to have kept you waiting.

Jenny: No worries, you're not that late. My daughter was an hour late for our meeting yesterday. She said she missed my message about the time change.

Tom: Oh wow! What did you do?

Jenny: I said that I hoped it wouldn't happen again.

Dialogue #2:

Tim: My bad. Sorry for not finishing my part of the assignment on time.

Carrie: You put us in a tough spot.

Tim: I'm really sorry. How can I make it up to you?

Carrie: I think that if you finish your part by tomorrow morning, we can still turn it in on time.

Tim: Okay. I won't go to sleep until it's done.

Phrasal Verbs #2: Conned Out Of

Terry is talking to his friend about getting ripped off.

Terry: So I just got **conned out of** $1000! This salesman guy on *Craigslist* tricked me into buying a TV that doesn't even work.

Lauren: **Hang on**. Did you report it to the police?

Terry: No. I feel embarrassed about it. I didn't want to **come forward**.

Lauren: **Come on**. It won't take long to **fill out** the form at the police station. They see this kind of thing all the time. I'll **go with** you. I hate seeing you get screwed out of that much cash.

Terry: You're right. Let's **get it over with**. Maybe I can get some justice.

Vocabulary

conned out of: Tricked; fooled.

hang on: Wait.

come forward: Report something.

come on: Encouragement to do something.

fill out: Write information on a form.

go with: Join together.

get it over with: Do something that you don't want to do.

Practice

1. My grandpa was _____ his life-savings.

2. You have to _____ and report that guy!

3. Taxes! Let's just _____ now.

4. Please _____ this form and we'll get back to you if we're interested.

5. _____ a second. This is important. What's that website URL again?

6. Why don't I _____ you? It won't be so bad then. We'll grab some *Starbucks* before we go too.

7. _____. Keep going! You're almost there.

Answers

1. conned out of

2. come forward

3. get it over with

4. fill out

5. hang on

6. go with

7. come on

Time Expressions #2: Holiday Season

Tom runs into Nancy at the shopping mall after not seeing her for a long time.

Tom: Nancy! Hi. **Long time, no see**.

Nancy: It has been **a while**.

Tom: Wasn't it last **holiday season**? I think I was doing some **last-minute** shopping.

Nancy: I'm sure you're right. It must have been. I'm famous for shopping on **Christmas Eve.** What's up with you?

Tom: Same old, same old. Busy at work. Doing stuff with the kids. The usual. How about you?

Nancy: Oh, I got a new job at ABC Law. It's going well.

Tom: Congratulations!

Vocabulary

long time, no see: An expression you can say to someone if you haven't seen them in a few months or a year.

a while: Not a short time period.

holiday season: Generally refers to November and December in North America, Europe and other places around the world.

last-minute: At the last possible time.

Christmas Eve: The evening of December 24th.

same old, same old: An expression to say that nothing has changed since the last time talking.

Practice

1. Hey Ted! What's up? Oh, _____.

2. Judy! _____. Why haven't you been at soccer lately?

3. Things are so different this _____ because of Covid-19.

4. My family loves watching Home Alone on _____.

5. It's going to be _____ before dinner. If you're hungry, why don't you have a snack?

6. I have to do some _____ things for work. Can I call you in about an hour?

Answers

1. same old, same old

2. long time, no see

3. holiday season

4. Christmas Eve

5. a while

6. last-minute

Vocabulary #3

Cash

Meaning: Physical money (coins and bills).

Examples:

Does anyone carry *cash* these days?

I'll pay with *cash*, please.

Sorry, we don't take *cash*. Credit cards only.

Catch a cold

Meaning: Get sick with a runny hose, sore throat, headache, fever, cough, etc. Caught a cold = past tense.

Examples:

I can't come to work today. I *caught a cold*.

I'm scared of *catching a cold* from my sick husband.

I *caught a terrible cold* last year and it lasted for a month.

Catch my breath

Meaning: Stop and take a break after a busy period.

Examples:

Give me a minute to *catch my breath*.

Are you okay? Sit down and *catch your breath*.

I need a vacation to *catch my breath*. I've been working non-stop for months now.

Check out
Meaning: Have a look at something.

Examples:

Do you want to *check out* that new Italian restaurant this weekend?

Let's *check out* that James Bond movie tonight.

Did you *check out* that wine festival last weekend?

Chill out
Meaning: Relax; take a break.

Examples:

Hey, *chill out*. You don't need to get angry about this!

I'm going to just *chill out* at home this weekend. I've been so busy working lately.

I go for a walk outside when I need to *chill out*.

Chores
Meaning: Things someone has to do around the house. For example, clean the bathroom or do laundry.

Examples:

My favourite *chore* is washing dishes but I hate vacuuming.

What *chores* do you want to do this week? You need to choose two.

Let's finish our *chores* on Saturday morning and then we can go out and have fun.

Clean up
Meaning: Tidy; clean.

Examples:

Clean up your room!

Let's *clean up* the garage this weekend.

Can you help me *clean up* the kitchen?

Coffee date

Meaning: Meeting with someone over coffee. Can be romantic, or not.

Examples:

We should have a *coffee date* soon.

Can we schedule a *coffee date* for next week?

Ask her out on a *coffee date*. I think she'll say yes.

Concession

Meaning: A place where you can buy snacks or drinks at a sports event, movie theater, etc.

Examples:

I'm hungry! Let's go to the *concession.*

Is there a *concession* here? Let's get some lunch.

There's nothing healthy at this *concession.* I'll just eat when we get home.

Practice

cash, catch my breath, check out, chill out, clean up, coffee date, concession

1. Let's _____ at home this weekend. I'm so tired.

2. I need to take a break to _____.

3. Please _____ your dishes from breakfast.

4. Is there a _____ here? Let's get a snack for the game.

5. How was your _____?

6. Do you have _____ on you? They don't take credit cards.

Answers

1. chill out

2. catch my breath

3. clean up

4. concession

5. coffee date

6. cash

Dialogue #3: A Fun Weekend

Kara and Casey are talking about what they did on the weekend.

Kara: Hey Casey. Did you have a good weekend?

Casey: The best. How about you?

Kara: Same here. What did you do?

Casey: Well, the weather was great so I went to the beach all of Saturday and brought my paddleboard too. What did you get up to?

Kara: I went to the Sufjan Stevens concert. Amazing.

Casey: I heard about that but I couldn't get tickets in time. I'm happy you had a good time.

Check Your Understanding

1. What did Casey do on the weekend?

2. What did Kara do on the weekend?

3. How was the weather on Saturday?

Answers

1. She went to the beach.

2. She went to a concert.

3. The weather was nice on Saturday.

Story #3: The Boy Who Cried Wolf

Once, in a small village, a boy named Sam watched over sheep. Sam thought it was funny to yell, "Wolf!" and **trick** the **villagers**. They ran to help, but there was no wolf.

Sam did it again, and the villagers were upset. Later, a real wolf came. When Sam called for help, the villagers didn't believe him. The wolf hurt the sheep.

Sam learned to tell the truth. The story teaches us that being honest is important, so people trust us when we really need help.

The Moral

The moral of the story is that it's important to tell the truth. If we don't tell the truth, people might not believe us when we really need help. Being honest is the right thing to do.

Vocabulary

trick: Deceive or outwit.

villagers: People who live in a village (small town).

Comprehension Questions

1. Why did Sam shout "Wolf! Wolf!" the first time?

2. How did the villagers respond to Sam's first and second cries for help?

3. What happened when a real wolf came to the village?

4. What did Sam learn from the villagers' reaction to his pranks?

5. What is the moral of the story?

Answers

1. Sam shouted to trick the villagers.

2. The villagers rushed to help when Sam shouted about the wolf, but they were disappointed when they found out it was a trick the second time.

3. When a real wolf came, Sam shouted for help, but the villagers didn't believe him. The wolf attacked the sheep.

4. Sam learned that being honest is important.

5. The moral of the story is that it's important to tell the truth.

Expressions #3

Can I turn the TV on?

Oh sure, no problem.

Actually, I'd rather listen to music I think.

Do you mind if I turn up the music?

No, go ahead.

It's already quite loud!

Is it okay if I take the car to school tomorrow?

No, sorry. I need it for work.

Sure, no problem.

I'm planning on staying at my friend's house tonight? What do you think?

That's fine.

Don't you have school tomorrow?

Can I turn in my assignment three days late?

No, the deadline can't be changed.

Maybe, why do you need to?

Would it be all right if I took a look at your notes?

Sure, no problem.

Oh, they're so messy.

Dialogue #1:

Tom: Do you mind if I turn up the music? I can't hear that well in my old age!

Jenny: No, go ahead. It's fine with me.

Tom: And, I'd love to turn the heat up a bit too. It's freezing in here.

Jenny: Oh Tom, so many problems!

Dialogue #2:

Tim: Hey Mom, can I stay at Tony's house tonight?

Carrie: Are his parents going to be home?

Tim: Of course.

Carrie: It is a school night though, right?

Tim: No, remember it's a holiday tomorrow.

Carrie: Oh, that's right. Sure, you can. I'll just give his parents a quick call first though.

Phrasal Verbs #3: Burst Out

Zeke is telling his friend Ted about something that happened at work.

Ted: How was your day?

Zeke: Okay. So the craziest thing happened at work today! We were in a meeting and our boss **called on** Tommy to ask him his opinion about something. But, he was **dozing off.** He **woke up** and let out the biggest snort!

Ted: **Come on**. That didn't happen, did it? I don't believe you.

Zeke: For real. Why would I **make it up**? I almost **fell out** of my chair. I was laughing so hard. I don't think I can **get over** it. Every time I see Tommy now, I want to laugh.

Ted: What did your boss do?

Zeke: He was cool and just **burst out** laughing. We've all caught Tommy sleeping before but he's so good at his job that he can get away with it.

Vocabulary

called on: Asked someone to speak in class or at a meeting.

dozing off: Sleeping lightly.

woke up: Stopped sleeping.

come on: An expression that you can say when you don't believe someone.

make it up: Saying something that isn't true.

fell out: Came off of something.

get over it: Forget; forgive.

burst out: Make a loud noise.

Practice

1. Getting _____ in class is my worst nightmare.

2. I _____ late this morning and had to rush to get to work on time.

3. I _____ laughing at the coffee shop when my friend told a joke. It was so embarrassing.

4. My son _____ of his crib when he was little but thankfully, no serious injuries.

5. _____. Let's get real. I don't think we can do all those things in two hours.

6. My brother is the master of _____ on airplanes. I wish!

7. You'll _____ eventually. Have a beer with me tonight and let's not talk about it!

8. Why would he _____? It has to be true.

Answers

1. called on

2. woke up

3. burst out

4. fell out

5. come on

6. dozing off

7. get over it

8. make it up

Time Expressions #3: When I'm Sleeping

Bob and Sammy are talking about sleep problems.

Bob: Hey Sammy, what's up? Are you okay?

Sammy: I'm so tired **these days**.

Bob: Are you not getting enough sleep?

Sammy: I get a decent amount of sleep. **When I'm sleeping**, I think I must be restless or something. Like **when I wake up**, I feel okay but **by the afternoon**, I'm so exhausted.

Bob: **How many** hours are you getting?

Sammy: Oh, **7 hours a night**.

Bob: **What time** do you go to sleep?

Sammy: Around 10.

Bob: And do you have any alcohol or caffeine **in the evening**?

Sammy: Oh yeah, I usually have a few beers **before** I hit the sack to help me sleep.

Bob: Did you know that alcohol prevents your body from going into a deep sleep?

Vocabulary

these days: Recently.

when I'm sleeping: The period of time when someone is sleeping. For example, 11 pm to 7 am.

when I wake up: The point in time when someone goes from sleeping to being awake.

by the afternoon: A point in time before afternoon (around 1 pm).

7 hours a night: How many hours someone sleeps each evening.

what time: Asking about a specific time. For example, 10:30 or 7 pm.

in the evening: Some point during the nighttime hours. (approx 6 pm to midnight).

before: Preceding something.

Practice

1. Let's clean up the dishes _____ we go out.

2. _____, I usually spend a few minutes on my cellphone.

3. I generally sleep for _____.

4. _____, I'm looking for a new job. Hopefully something pans out soon.

5. _____, I like to be outside if the weather is nice.

6. I'm usually desperate for more coffee _____.

7. I like to have some background noise like a fan on _____. I live on a busy street.

8. _____ are we meeting at the restaurant again?

Answers

1. before

2. when I wake up

3. 7 hours a night

4. these days

5. in the evening

6. by the afternoon

7. when I'm sleeping

8. what time

Vocabulary #4

Cook dinner
Meaning: Make food for an evening meal.

Example:

What should we *cook for dinner* tonight?

I don't feel like *cooking dinner*. Let's go out tonight.

Can you *cook dinner* for the kids today? I won't be home until after 6:00.

Co-workers
Meaning: People that work together.

Examples:

Do you like your *co-workers*?

I only have four *co-workers*. I work at a small company.

I don't know all my *co-workers*. There are hundreds of people in my building.

Cut back on
Meaning: Reduce; consume or use less.

Examples:

I want to *cut back on* drinking beer this year.

We need to *cut back on* eating out. It's too expensive.

I don't want to keep using credit cards. Let's c*ut back on* going out.

Day off
Meaning: Not working or going to school.

Examples:

What do you like to do on your *day off*?

I don't have many *days off* from work and school.

Sunday and Monday are my *days off*.

Dinner party

Meaning: A gathering where the host cooks dinner for everyone.

Examples:

I'm going to a *dinner party* tonight at Eric's house.

Let's have a *dinner party* next month.

I love hosting *dinner parties.*

Downtown

Meaning: The center of a city, usually with tall office buildings.

Examples:

There's lots of traffic *downtown*.

I work *downtown*. There are lots of good restaurants and bars.

Living *downtown* is so expensive in Vancouver.

Dress up

Meaning: Wear something nice (for example, at a wedding), or unusual (for example, at Halloween).

Examples:

Are you going to *dress up* for Halloween?

Let's *dress up* and go for a nice dinner tonight.

Do I have to *dress up* for your work party?

Practice

cook dinner, co-workers, day off, cut back on, downtown, dinner party, dress up

1. Ted is having a _____ and he invited me.

2. What are you going to do on your _____?

3. My _____ are terrible. They are so lazy.

4. I'm going to _____ now. I'll talk to you later.

5. I want to _____ on eating out to save some money.

6. Do you like living _____?

7. Do I need to _____ for the party?

Answers

1. dinner party

2. day off

3. co-workers

4. cook dinner

5. cut back on

6. downtown

7. dress up

Dialogue #4: Taking the Bus

Ted and Chris are trying to figure out how to get to the airport from downtown.

Ted: How are we going to get to the airport tomorrow?

Chris: Isn't there a bus that goes there?

Ted: Probably. Do you know which one?

Chris: I think number seven is the airport bus but let's check online and see.

Ted: Sure, I have my computer right here.

Chris: Perfect.

Ted: Okay. It is the number seven. It leaves every twenty minutes and the stop is just a few minutes away from here. Let's try to get the 1:20? That leaves us plenty of time.

Chris: Sounds like a plan.

Check Your Understanding

1. Where are they going?

2. How often does the airport bus run?

3. Where is the bus stop?

Answers

1. They are going to the airport.

2. The bus runs every twenty minutes.

3. The bus stop is only a few minutes away.

Story #4: The Fox and the Crow

Once in a forest, there was a clever fox and a curious crow with a piece of cheese. The fox wanted the cheese, so he said to the crow, "Crow, you're a fantastic singer! Can you sing for me?"

The crow felt happy and started to sing. While singing, the crow opened its **beak**, and the cheese fell down. The fox quickly grabbed it and said, "Thank you for the song!" and ran away.

The lesson is to be careful and not believe everything people say, especially if they want something from you.

The Moral

The moral of the story is to be careful and not believe everything people say, especially if they want something from you. It teaches us to be cautious and not let flattery or kind words cloud our judgment.

Vocabulary

beak: The nose of a bird.

clever: Smart; intelligent.

curious: Eager to know or learn about something.

Comprehension Questions

1. Why did the fox approach the crow?

2. What did the fox compliment the crow on?

3. What did the crow do when the fox asked it to sing?

4. What happened while the crow was singing?

5. How did the fox get the cheese?

Answers

1. The fox approached the crow because it wanted the crow's cheese.

2. The fox complimented the crow on his singing.

3. The crow opened its beak.

4. While the crow was singing, the piece of cheese fell from its beak to the ground below.

5. The fox took advantage of the crow's singing, grabbed the cheese, and thanked the crow before running away.

Expressions #4

Could you open the window/door, please?

Sure.

Of course.

Certainly.

Could you make me a cup of tea, please?

No problem.

Could you please give me a hand?

Sure, what do you need?

Could you look after my daughter this weekend?

Sorry, I can't. I'm really busy.

Yes, I can.

Do you mind moving so that we could sit together?

Oh sure, no problem.

Do you have a few extra dollars to spare?

Sorry, I'm flat broke.

Sure, what's going on?

Do you have an extra pen I could borrow?

Sorry, I only have this one.

Yes, here you go.

Dialogue #1:

50

Tom: Could you please give me a hand this weekend?

Jenny: Sure, what do you need?

Tom: Would you mind looking after Tony during my dentist appointment?

Jenny: Okay, no problem. I love hanging out with him. What time?

Tom: From 2 until around 4.

Dialogue #2:

Tim: Oh hi, excuse me. Do you mind moving over one seat so that my friend and I could sit together?

Carrie: Sure, no problem.

Tim: Thanks so much.

Carrie: Of course, enjoy the movie.

Phrasal Verbs #4: Come Over

Ethan and Allan are talking about hanging out after work.

Ethan: Hey, do you want to **come over** after work today for a beer?

Allan: Sure I'll **drop in** on my way home. I would love to **kick back**. It's been a long week.

Ethan: Well, **let yourself in**. I'll be on the patio around back. I might **ring up** Tony too and see if he can join us.

Allan: Sure Oh yeah. I'll **stop by** the bank and **pick up** some cash. I have to pay you back for last weekend.

Ethan: That's right. Okay. We'll **figure it out.**

Vocabulary

come over: Visit at someone's house.

drop in: Visit someone, or do something without making a specific appointment.

kick back: Relax.

let yourself in: Don't ring the doorbell but come into a house yourself (when invited to do so).

ring up: Call.

stop by: Visit at someone's home or business.

pick up: Get something.

figure it out: Come to an understanding; solve something.

Practice

1. Why don't you _____ on Tuesday for dinner?

2. Can you please _____ a pizza for dinner tonight?

3. You're here now! Just _____ and have a beer.

4. Please _____. It's difficult to hear the doorbell.

5. Don't worry about it. We'll _____ together.

6. I'll _____ after dinner tonight. Is that okay?

7. You can just _____ between six and nine. No need to make an appointment.

8. Let's _____ Tony. We haven't seen him in a long time.

Answers

1. come over

2. pick up

3. kick back

4. let yourself in

5. figure it out

6. stop by

7. drop in

8. ring up

Time Expressions #4: From Dawn Till Dusk

Mandy is talking to Eric about how her work is going.

Eric: How's work going **these days**?

Mandy: Same old, same old. I have to work **from dawn till dusk**. We have all these deadlines from clients and are always **running out of time**.

Eric: Can you reduce your hours? That's terrible not having any **free time**.

Mandy: Not if I want to **get ahead** in this industry. I'd love to **take my time** on projects and not be **in a rush** too. But, that's **not going to cut it**.

Vocabulary

these days: Lately.

same old, same old: Nothing has changed.

from dawn till dusk: Working very long hours (early morning to late at night).

running out of time: Lacking time to finish or do something.

free time: Leisure time when not working or studying.

get ahead: Make gains, especially compared to other people.

take my time: Not hurry.

in a rush: The need to do something quickly.

not going to cut it: Something you do isn't good enough.

Practice

1. Please do it again. That's _____.

2. In my _____, I love to hang out with friends.

3. He's always _____ with his math homework and gets so many answers wrong.

4. I have to work _____ during the year-end.

5. Covid-19 has impacted my social life! It's _____ around here.

6. I'd love to _____ and make a good decision about which program to take.

7. It's difficult to _____ in Vancouver when housing is so expensive.

8. _____, I'm trying to get in better shape.

9. We're _____ and will need to stay late tonight.

Answers

1. not going to cut it

2. free time

3. in a rush

4. from dawn till dusk

5. same old, same old

6. take my time

7. get ahead

8. these days

9. running out of time

Vocabulary #5

Flyers

Meaning: Paper advertisements that are delivered to houses.

Examples:

Does anyone look at *flyers*?

I hate getting all these *flyers*.

Have a look at the *flyers*. I want to buy a new TV. Let's see if there are any sales.

Free

Meaning: Describes something that doesn't cost any money.

Examples:

I got a *free* couch this weekend from my friend who was moving.

It's so cheap it's almost *free*!

I need to find a new bed for *free*. Mine broke but I don't have any money.

Free time

Meaning: Leisure time when not working or studying.

Examples:

What do you like to do in your *free time*?

I don't have much *free time* since I had kids.

In my *free time*, I love to play sports with friends.

Fruits and vegetables

Meaning: Fruits (banana, apple, etc.) and vegetables (carrot, onion, etc.).

Examples:

I want to eat more *fruits and vegetables* this year.

My kids hate *fruits and vegetables*.

I love all kinds of *fruits and vegetables*, except for bananas and eggplant.

Get online

Meaning: Use the Internet.

Examples:

How do you *get online*?

Is there a way that we can help seniors *get online*?

How can I *get online* here? Is there a WiFi password?

Get serious

Meaning: Start taking something more seriously.

Examples:

I need to *get serious* about saving money.

Let's *get serious* about getting in shape!

You need to *get serious* about school. You're failing math.

Get together with

Meaning: See; hang out with.

Examples:

We should *get together with* Jill and Cayla next weekend.

Let's *get together with* your parents soon.

It's been a while. Let's *get together with* our families soon.

Give up

Meaning: Stop trying; quit/stop using something.

Examples:

I'm trying to *give up* smoking.

Don't *give up*! You can do it.

I know you want to *give up* but you only have 3 more classes and then you'll be done.

Good sense of humour

Meaning: Describes someone who likes to laugh and tell jokes. No sense of humour = opposite.

Examples:

Does your teacher have a *good sense of humour*?

My boyfriend has a *good sense of humour*.

She has *no sense of humour*.

Good with computers

Meaning: Describes someone who knows how to use computers well.

Examples:

Are you *good with computers*?

Everyone calls me to help them because I'm *good with computers*.

I'm not *good with computers*. I always have to call my son.

Practice

flyers, good with computers, free time, get serious, fruit and vegetables, get online, give up, get along with, good sense of humour

1. Do you know anyone who is _____? I need some help.

2. What do you like to do in your _____?

3. I want to eat more _____.

4. _____. We can't finish that by tonight.

5. Don't _____! I know you can pass that test if you study.

6. It's difficult for seniors to _____.

7. Do you _____ your co-workers?

8. I want to date somebody with a _____.

Answers

1. good with computers

2. free time

3. fruit and vegetables

4. Get serious

5. give up

6. get online

7. get along with

8. good sense of humour

59

Dialogue #5: Playing Tennis

Ted and Sam are making plans to play tennis.

Ted: Hey, do you want to play tennis on Sunday?

Sam: I'd love to. Where do you usually play?

Ted: At Gates Park. What about meeting there at 1:00?

Sam: That sounds perfect. I'll see you then.

Ted: Should we invite two more people or play singles?

Sam: Let's play singles. I need a good run.

Ted: Okay. I should get more exercise too!

Check Your Understanding

1. Where are they playing tennis?

2. How many people are playing?

3. When are they playing?

Answers

1. They are playing tennis at Gates Park.

2. Two people are playing.

3. They are playing on Sunday at 1:00.

Story #5: A Council of Mice

Once in a field, there were many little mice. They were happy until a cat named Whiskers started chasing and **catching** them. The mice got scared and didn't know what to do.

The smartest mouse, Whiskerington, called a meeting. They talked about how to stay safe. A brave mouse, Squeaky, said, "Let's tell each other when Whiskers is close, and we can hide."

Another mouse, Swift, had an idea too. "Let's build **hiding spots** to hide quickly if Whiskers comes." The mice liked these ideas, so they started telling each other and built hiding spots. It worked! Whiskers couldn't catch them anymore, and the mice felt safe.

The story teaches us that when we work together and use our brains, we can solve problems and stay safe, even from something scary like a cat.

The Moral

The moral of the story is that when we work together and use our brains, we can solve problems and stay safe, even from something scary like a cat. Teamwork and clever thinking help us overcome challenges.

Vocabulary

catching: Capturing.

hiding spots: Places where someone or something can't be found.

Comprehension Questions

1. What was the problem that the mice faced in the story?

2. Who was the leader of the mice?

3. What were the two ideas the mice decided to use to stay safe from Whiskers?

4. Did the plan of the mice work against Whiskers? How?

5. What does the story teach us about solving problems?

Answers

1. The mice faced a problem of being caught by a cat named Whiskers.

2. Whiskerington was the leader of the mice.

3. The mice decided to warn each other when Whiskers was close and to build safe hiding spots.

4. Yes, the plan worked. By warning each other and having safe hiding spots, Whiskers couldn't catch the mice anymore.

5. The story teaches us that working together can help us solve problems and stay safe.

Expressions #5

Let's open the window. It's so hot in here!

Good idea.

Oh, I have the air conditioning on. I'll just turn it up a little bit for you.

Why don't we ask my Mom to look after Jenny this weekend?

That's a great idea.

Oh, she's going camping this weekend with her friends.

How about taking the subway there?

I'd prefer to drive. It's so crowded at this time of day.

Sounds good.

What about checking out that new Italian place tonight?

Sounds great.

I just had Italian last night. What about Chinese?

Can we stop going out so much? I'm short on cash these days.

Oh definitely. Let's eat at home tonight.

I'd recommend checking out Stanley Park when you go to Vancouver.

Thank you. I'll have a look at that.

Have you thought about just getting a new computer?

Yeah, I have but they're so expensive. I'm hoping to just fix this one.

Oh really? That might be something to consider.

Dialogue #1:

Tom: I want to do something fun this weekend! Why don't we ask your parents to look after Tony?

Jenny: That's a great idea. How about checking out that new Greek restaurant?

Tom: Sounds good. I'll give your parents a call and see what they say.

Jenny: Perfect.

Dialogue #2:

Tim: Hey Carrie, do you want to catch a movie this weekend?

Carrie: Honestly, I'm a little short on cash these days. How about staying in and watching a movie at my house?

Tim: Sure, that sounds great too. There's this new one that just came out on Netflix that everyone is talking about.

Carrie: Awesome! I'll make some snacks for us. Come over at 7:30.

Phrasal Verbs #5: Dry Out

Keith and Ken are talking about cleaning up after their camping trip.

Keith: Ugggh...I hate **packing up** camp in the rain! But, we're almost home so let's **think ahead** about how we're going to unpack.

Ken: Good idea. Well, we need to **dry out** the tent so let's work together to hang it up. Oh, and let's **plug in** our phones first. They're both dead I think, right?

Keith: I can **take in** all the food and **wipe out** the cooler after that.

Ken: Sure. And I'll **look up** the number for that pizza place we like! I'm so hungry for real food. I can order something and by the time it arrives, we'll hopefully be done unpacking.

Vocabulary

packing up: Gathering all your belongings and putting them together.

think ahead: Make a plan or consider something in advance.

dry out: Expose wet things to the air so that they won't be wet.

plug in: What do you with an electrical device when you want to use it not with a battery.

take in: Bring something inside.

wipe out: Clean.

look up: Find some information.

Practice

1. I love camping but _____ all the gear at the end of the trip is the worst.

2. Don't forget to _____ the sink after you're done with the dishes.

3. Where can I _____ my computer? There are no outlets in this classroom.

4. Take your wet socks out of your shoes or they'll never _____.

5. Let's _____ about how we're going to tackle this. It's a big project.

6. I can _____ what date the campground opens.

7. Can you please _____ your bag when we get home? I'll grab the soccer ball.

Answers

1. packing up

2. wipe out

3. plug in

4. dry out

5. think ahead

6. look up

7. take in

Time Expressions #5: For the Time Being

Sid and Ho-Hyun are talking about how busy they are (or aren't).

Sid: What's up these days Ho-Hyun?

Ho-Hyun: Did you hear? I lost my job because of Covid last month. The restaurant I'm working at closed. I have a lot of **time on my hands** these days.

Sid: So what do you do?

Ho-Hyun: **For the time being**, I'm just enjoying myself. I **rarely** have time to do that as a chef. I **pass the time of day** with my neighbor, watch some Netflix and try to go for a walk every day. What are you up to?

Sid: **At the moment**, I'm also looking for work. I **still** have my old job but I don't really like it that much. I'm seeing what else is out there. **Formerly**, it was okay but my boss left and the new guy is terrible.

Ho-Hyun: Sorry to hear that.

Vocabulary

time on my hands: Lots of free time.

for the time being: At the present time.

rarely: Not often.

pass the time of day: Chit-chat with someone to kill time.

at the moment: These days.

still: Up to, and including the present time.

formerly: Previously.

Practice

1. _____, I was a teacher.

2. _____, I'm working at Home Depot but I hope to get a better job.

3. I'm so bored at work. My coworker and I just _____ for hours.

4. I _____ drink alcohol

5. I have a lot of _____. Maybe I'll clean out the garage this weekend.

6. I _____ have some lingering side effects from getting Covid-19.

Answers

1. formerly

2. for the time being/at the moment

3. pass the time of day

4. rarely

5. time on my hands

6. still

Vocabulary #6

Good with money

Meaning: Someone who knows how to handle money well.

Examples:

Tom is *good with money.* Why don't you ask him for some advice?

I wish I was *good with money*! I'm tired of being broke.

It's not impossible to be *good with money.* Just stop buying things!

Government

Meaning: The group of people in charge of a city, state/province or country.

Examples:

The *government* is doing a terrible job running my city.

The Canadian *government* changes every 4-5 years.

There are many *government* offices near where I live.

Hang on

Meaning: Wait.

Examples:

Hang on a minute. Let me take a look.

Hang on. I need a few minutes to eat dinner before we go.

Can you *hang on*? I'm not ready to go yet.

Hang out

Meaning: Spend time in a relaxed way.

Examples:

Do you want to *hang out* this weekend?

I'm *hanging out* with Tommy this weekend.

I like to *hang out* in coffee shops.

Hangover
Meaning: Feeling sick because of drinking too much the night before.

Examples:

Ughhh...I have a terrible *hangover*.

I never used to get *hangovers* when I was younger.

No more beer. I don't want to have a *hangover* tomorrow. I have to work.

Happily married
Meaning: A good marriage.

Examples:

Tony and I are *happily married.*

Do you think Tim and Sarah are *happily married*? They fight all the time.

I was *happily married* for 10 years but then my wife died.

Have a drink
Meaning: Drink alcohol.

Examples:

Do you want to *have a drink* after work?

Let's *have a drink* this weekend.

I like to *have a drink* on Friday nights.

Practice

good with money, hangover, hang out, hang on, government, happily married, have a drink

1. I've been _____ for 10 years.

2. You should _____. That cough sounds terrible.

3. I went hiking but I _____. It was a long day!

4. I never used to get a _____ when I was in university.

5. Isn't Tony _____? Let's ask him for some advice.

6. Do you want to _____ this weekend?

Answers

1. happily married

2. hang on

3. hangover

4. good with money

5. hang out

Dialogue #6: Getting Information from the Bus Driver

Johnny wants to find out some information from the bus driver.

Johnny: Does this bus go downtown?

Bus Driver: No, you'll need to take the number six instead.

Johnny: Oh, okay. Can I catch it at this bus stop?

Bus Driver: You'll want to cross the street and take the bus in the other direction.

Johnny: Okay. Great. Thank you. Oh, do you know how often it runs?

Bus Driver: I don't know exactly but there are a lot of them. During rush hour, maybe every 10 minutes.

Check Your Understanding

1. Where does Johnny want to go?

2. Which bus goes downtown?

3. How often does the bus run at 2:00 in the afternoon?

Answers

1. He wants to go downtown.

2. The #6 bus goes downtown.

3. Not enough information. We only know about rush hour.

Story #6: The Frightened Lion

Once in a big field, there was a lion named Leo. Leo was very strong but scared of buzzing bees, loud thunder, and tiny mice. Leo's friends, other animals, noticed he was always scared. An old elephant named Ella said, "Why are you afraid, Leo? You're strong!"

Leo said, "Bees, thunder, and mice make me nervous." His friends helped Leo face his fears. They showed him bees are busy, thunder is just noise, and mice are more scared of him.

Leo felt **braver** and thanked his friends. Now, he wasn't scared anymore and **roared** confidently. The story teaches us that sometimes our fears aren't as big as we think, and with friends' help, we can be brave.

The Moral

The moral of the story is that sometimes things that seem scary are not really as big as we think. With help from friends, we can be brave and face our fears.

Vocabulary

braver: More ready to face danger.

roared: Made a big noise (from a lion).

Comprehension Questions

1. What scared Leo the lion in the story?

2. Who noticed that Leo was always scared?

3. How did Leo's friends help him face his fear of bees?

4. What did Leo learn about thunderstorms?

5. What made Leo feel braver in the end?

Answers

1. Leo was scared of bees, thunderstorms, and mice.

2. The other animals in the jungle noticed that he was always scared.

3. They showed Leo that bees are busy and won't bother him.

4. Leo learned that thunderstorms are just loud noises.

5. Leo felt braver in the end because his friends showed him that the things he was scared of were not as big as he thought.

Expressions #6

My grandfather had a heart attack last night.

Oh, that's terrible.

I'm here for you if you want to talk.

My back hurts so much.

Sorry to hear that. Anything I can do to help?

I lost my jacket.

Let me help you look for it.

When did you last have it?

I've wasted half an hour looking for my car keys.

Oh no!

Can I help you look for them?

I have a really bad cold.

Take care of yourself, okay?

Please let me know if you need anything.

My boyfriend just broke up with me.

Oh no, please let me know if you want to talk.

Let's get some ice cream, okay?

Dialogue #1:

Tom: I got some sad news last night. I heard that my grandmother died.

Jenny: Oh no, I'm so sorry to hear that.

Tom: Yes, me too. We weren't that close but I'll miss her.

Jenny: Anything I can do to help? Want to grab a coffee and talk?

Dialogue #2:

Tim: Do you want to go for a quick hike after work today?

Carrie: Oh, I can't. I have a terrible cold.

Tim: Oh no! Did you stay home from work today?

Carrie: Yes. For the past three days actually.

Tim: Oh friend. That's terrible. Do you need me to bring you anything?

Carrie: My Mom brought me over some homemade soup. I'm doing okay.

Phrasal Verbs #6: Build In

Keith and Jen are talking about what their plans are for the weekend.

Keith: Should we talk about our weekend plans?

Jen: Sure, my main priority is **staying up** to watch the Oilers and then **getting up** late the next day. But let's **build in** some time for cleaning and organizing too. Our house is getting so messy.

Keith: I **figured on** that. Let's do a deep clean. And also **put together** that new coffee table. We've been so lazy.

Jen: Let's do it. And what about food? We have that soup from yesterday we can **heat up** for a couple of meals but we'll need to **pick up** groceries.

Keith: Sure thing.

Vocabulary

staying up: Going to bed later than the usual time.

getting up: Waking up.

build in: Allow time for.

figured on: Already knew.

put together: Assemble.

heat up: Make something warm.

pick up: Get something or someone from somewhere.

Practice

1. The kids have been _____ so late during summer vacation.

2. I'll _____ some Thai on my way home from work.

3. I _____ that. I just wanted to check and see if you'd changed your mind.

4. Can you help me _____ my new dresser today?

5. Let's _____ some time to chill out this weekend. We've been so busy these days.

6. _____ early is so difficult for me.

7. Let's _____ the stew for dinner.

Answers

1. staying up

2. pick up

3. figured on

4. put together

5. build in

6. getting up

7. heat up

Time Expressions #6: Every Winter

Katie and Kim are talking about the first snow of the year.

Katie: Did you hear that it's going to snow **tomorrow evening**?

Kim: Really? That seems **earlier** than normal. I was hoping it wouldn't happen until **next month**.

Katie: I don't think so. Doesn't it always happen around Halloween **every year**?

Kim: You're right I guess. **Every winter**, I'm always happy **on the first day** of snow but then I hate it!

Katie: I don't mind. The kids love making snowmen and sledding. They spend more time outside when there's lots of snow.

Kim: True, but I'm the one who has to shovel the driveway!

Vocabulary

tomorrow evening: The next night.

earlier: Before, compared to something else.

next month: The following month. If it's May now, then June.

every year: Happens each year.

every winter: Happens each winter.

on the first day: The initial time something occurs.

Practice

1. _____ of summer, I love to celebrate with a backyard party.

2. With climate change, it seems like the snow is melting _____ each year.

3. _____, I like to plant my garden around May 1st.

4. _____, I love to plan a ski trip with my friends.

5. I'm going to start university _____.

6. Why don't we catch a movie _____?

Answers

1. on the first day

2. earlier

3. every year

4. every winter

5. next month

6. tomorrow evening

Vocabulary #7

Look after

Meaning: Take care of someone or something.

Examples:

Can you *look after* Tim on Friday night?

Do you have someone to *look after* the house when you're on vacation?

Who's *looking after* your cats when you're camping?

Lost and found

Meaning: A place to look for something that you've lost.

Examples:

Excuse me, do you have a *lost and found*? I left my guitar on the train yesterday.

Have you checked the *lost and found*? They have a lot of water bottles there.

I think we'll be able to find your jacket in the *lost and found.* Let's take a look.

Make Money

Meaning: Do a job, task, etc. to get paid.

Examples:

I want to *make money*! I have to get a part-time job.

I need to *make more money*. Vancouver is expensive.

If you want to *make money*, you need to get a job.

Map

Meaning: A picture showing locations and places.

Examples:

Is that a *map*? Let's see where that store is.

I use Google *Maps* all the time when I'm driving.

Let's stop and look at that *map*. I think we're lost

Minimum wage

Meaning: The minimum amount of money a job can legally pay (set by the government).

Examples:

The *minimum wage* in British Colombia is $16.20/hour.

I get paid *minimum wage*.

We need to increase the *minimum wage* in the U.S.A.

Practice

look after, make money, lost and found, map, minimum wage

1. I'll get a job this summer. I need to _____.

2. I wish the _____ were higher in the USA.

3. It's always a good idea to take a _____ when you go hiking.

4. Sorry, I have to go home right now. I need to _____ my kids.

5. Maybe your umbrella is in the _____?

Answers

1. make money

2. minimum wage

3. map

4. look after

5. lost and found

Dialogue #7: Help with an Assignment

Carrie is helping Tim with an assignment.

Tim: Carrie, I appreciate your help with that assignment.

Carrie: No problem, it was a tough one. It took me a long time to do it.

Tim: Yeah, I just couldn't figure it out. I spent 10 hours on it but made no progress.

Carrie: Anyway, I'm always happy to help a friend out. You've done the same for me many times!

Tim: I'm thankful to have you in this class with me.

Carrie: I feel the same way.

Check your Understanding

1. Is the assignment difficult?

2. How do Tim and Carrie know each other?

3. Is this the first time they've worked together on an assignment?

Answers

1. Yes, it's very difficult.

2. They are in the same class at school.

3. No, they've done it many times in the past.

Story #7: The Dog and His Reflection

Once in a little village, there was a dog named Max. Max had a shiny coat and a happy tail. One sunny day, Max saw another dog in a **pond**. He barked, and the other dog barked back. Max thought he found a new friend!

Excited, Max jumped into the pond. The other dog did the same. Max **wagged** his tail, and so did the other dog. Max thought it was the best playmate ever!

He played and danced, but then he noticed something strange. When he dropped a stick into the water, the other dog didn't give it back. Max realized it was just his reflection, not a real friend.

Max learned that he shouldn't be **fooled** by what he sees. Real friends share and play together. Now, when Max sees his **reflection**, he remembers to look for real friends who share sticks in the sunshine.

The moral is to know the difference between what's real and what's just a reflection. True friends share and play together.

The Moral

The moral of the story is to be careful not to be fooled by appearances. It's important to distinguish between what's real and what's just a reflection. True friends are the ones who share and play together, not just those who mimic our actions.

Vocabulary

pond: A small body of water (smaller than a lake).

wagged: Moved a tail of an animal around quickly.

fooled: Tricked.

reflection: An image seen on a shiny surface like water or a mirror.

Comprehension Questions

1. What did Max notice near the pond one sunny day?

2. Why did Max think he found a new friend?

3. What did Max realize when he dropped a stick into the water?

4. What lesson did Max learn from the experience?

5. How did Max feel when he discovered the truth about the water dog?

Answers

1. Max noticed another dog that looked just like him, but in the water.

2. Max thought he found a new friend because he saw the other dog in the water.

3. Max realized that the other dog in the water wasn't a real friend because it didn't give the stick back.

4. Max learned not to be tricked by appearances.

5. Max felt a silly when he realized the water dog was just his reflection.

Expressions #7

Can I exchange some money, please?

Of course. No problem. How much?

What currency would you like?

Euros, please.

Would you like big or small notes?

A mix of big and small bills, please.

Mostly small notes, please.

Sorry, we don't accept coins.

Oh, okay. Thank you.

Can you please show me your passport?

Okay.

Here's your money.

Thank you.

Dialogue:

Tom: Can I please exchange some money?

Jenny: Sure, how much and what currency?

Tom: I'd like to get Canadian dollars, please. $700.

Jenny: Okay, and can you please show me your passport as well?

Tom: Sure.

Jenny: Would you like a mix of big and small bills?

Tom: Yes, please. That sounds great.

Phrasal Verbs #7: Ran Into You

Carrie and Tim bumped into each other at the grocery store.

Tim: Carrie!

Carrie: Wow, **it's been a while**, right? Maybe a year?

Tim: Yeah, I think it was around Christmas last year that I **ran into you** at the mall. I was doing my **last-minute shopping**.

Carrie: That's right. **What's up** with you?

Tim: Just busy at work. Not much besides that. How about you?

Carrie: I got a new dog and we've been having so much fun with him.

Tim: Nice! Anyway, nice to see you again! I **gotta run pick up** Tony from soccer pretty soon.

Carrie: For sure. Let's **catch up** over coffee soon.

Vocabulary

it's been a while: Same as, "long time, no see."

ran into you: Saw in person, randomly.

last-minute shopping: Going shopping right before you need the present, usually before Christmas.

what's up: What's new?/How are you?

gotta run: I need to go now.

pick up: Get something or someone.

catch up: Share news about what's happening in our lives.

Practice

1. Let's _____ next week, okay?

2. _____ with you these days?

3. I'm so happy that I _____.

4. I _____. I need to get Tim in 10 minutes.

5. Can you _____ some milk on your way home?

6. Oh wow. _____, hasn't it?

7. I need to do some _____ for the party tomorrow.

Answers

1. catch up

2. what's up

3. ran into you

4. gotta run

5. pick up

6. it's been a while

7. last-minute shopping

Time Expressions #7: At Breakfast

Allen is complaining on the phone to his friend Terry about his son Nate who is a picky eater.

Terry: Allen? Hey, what's up?

Allen: **At this very moment**, I'm so angry at Nate. He's suddenly decided to become the world's pickiest eater.

Terry: What happened?

Allen: Well **at breakfast**, he decided he wasn't going to eat cereal anymore and that I should cook him eggs, pancakes or waffles **every day**. And then **at lunch**, he didn't want the pasta that I made.

Terry: Ohhh...that's frustrating.

Allen: It gets worse. **By the time** dinner came around, I was already fuming so I asked what he'd like. He said pizza, so I made his favourite kind—ham and pineapple. Then he sat down and said that he meant from the pizza shop. Not homemade pizza. I **seldom** yell but at that point, I told him to go to his room and that he couldn't have any dinner.

Terry: Oh no! How did it end?

Allen: Well, **later that evening**, he came down and apologized for being so difficult and asked if there was any leftover pizza.

Vocabulary

at this very moment: Right now.

at breakfast: During the morning meal.

every day: 7 days a week.

at lunch: During the midday meal.

by the time: A way to explain what has already happened when something else happens.

seldom: Rarely.

later that evening: After the point in time being talked about, at night.

Practice

1. I had a terrible day. First, I got my car broken into and then _____, I lost my keys.

2. _____, everyone is in such a rush that we rarely eat together.

3. I hang out with my coworkers _____.

4. I _____ drink alcohol, maybe just after playing golf.

5. I like to exercise _____.

6. _____, I'm getting ready to go to work. Can I call you later?

7. _____ you stop complaining about this, you could already be done!

Answers

1. later that evening

2. at breakfast

3. at lunch

4. seldom

5. every day

6. at this very moment

7. by the time

Vocabulary #8

I'm down

Meaning: An expression that shows you want to do the thing that the other person is suggesting. Same as, "I'm in."

Examples:

I'm down for drinks after work tomorrow, if you are?

Who's down for a hike this weekend?

Are you down for watching a movie on Friday?

Information

Meaning: Knowledge.

Examples:

The first step is research. You need more *information* about this situation.

Where's the *information* desk?

Do some research before buying a car. The more *information* you have, the better.

Invite

Meaning: Ask someone to do something.

Examples:

Do you want to *invite* a friend to a movie this weekend?

We should *invite* Carrie to go camping with us.

How many people are you going to *invite* to your wedding?

Job interview

Meaning: An interview between an employer and a potential employee.

Examples:

I have a *job interview* at 2:00 today.

What time is your *job interview*?

I have a few *job interviews* next week. Hopefully, I can get a job!

Junk food
Meaning: Food that isn't healthy.

Examples:

I eat so much *junk food!*

My teenagers love *junk food.* I worry about their health all the time.

I want to eat more fruits and vegetables this year and less *junk food.*

Keep a secret
Meaning: Not telling other people what someone told you.

Examples:

Can you *keep a secret*?

Tony is famous for not *keeping secrets.*

I'll tell you but only if you can *keep a secret.*

Kill time
Meaning: Do something to fill time. For example, when waiting for a bus or train.

Examples:

How do I like to *kill time*? I usually waste so much time playing Candy Crush!

We have *some time to kill* before we have to pick up Carrie. What do you want to do?

I like *killing time* at the airport before a flight. I get some food and have a drink.

Language
Meaning: Words (vocabulary), and how to combine them (grammar). Examples are English, French, Korean, Spanish, Mandarin, etc.

Examples:

Which *languages* do you speak?

I only speak one *language*—English.

I love to learn new *languages.*

Practice

Information, job interviews, I'm down, junk food, keep a secret, invite, kill time, languages

1. I don't think Ted can _____.

2. _____ for hiking this weekend. Saturday or Sunday?

3. Kara can speak seven _____.

4. How do you like to _____?

5. Should we _____ Jen over for dinner?

6. I used to eat so much _____ but my doctor told me to cut back.

7. I have three _____ next week.

Answers

1. keep a secret

2. I'm down

3. languages

4. kill time

5. invite

6. junk food

7. job interviews

Dialogue #8: Bumping into Someone

Carrie and Tim bumped into each other at the grocery store.

Tim: Carrie! Long time, no see.

Carrie: Wow, it has been a while, right? Maybe a year?

Tim: Yeah, I think it was around Christmas last year that I ran into you at the mall.

Carrie: That's right. I remember that. How are you?

Tim: Oh good. Just busy at work. Nothing new. How about you?

Carrie: I got a new dog and we've been having so much fun with him.

Tim: Nice! Anyway, nice to see you again! I gotta run pick up Tony from soccer pretty soon.

Carrie: For sure. Let's catch up over coffee soon.

Check your Understanding

1. When was the last time they saw each other?

2. Why can't Tim stay and talk?

3. Is Tim busy at work?

Answers

1. It was about a year ago.

2. He has to pick up his son at soccer soon.

3. Yes, he is.

Story #8: A Bundle of Sticks

Once in a village, there were five brothers and sisters who were always **arguing**. Their grandma wanted to teach them a lesson, so she told them a story.

Grandma gave each sibling a stick and asked them to break it. They easily broke their sticks. Then, she gave them a **bundle** of sticks tied together and asked them to break the bunch. They couldn't break it. Grandma said, "Alone, you break easily. Together, you are strong."

The **siblings** understood. They decided to stay together, help each other, and be strong. The village noticed the change, and the siblings became a happy family.

The lesson is that when people work together, they are stronger. Like a bunch of sticks is harder to break than one stick, being together helps us face challenges.

The Moral

The moral of the story is that when people work together and support each other, they become stronger. Like a bunch of sticks tied together is harder to break than a single stick, unity and cooperation help us face challenges and difficulties in life.

Vocabulary

siblings: 2 or more children sharing a mother and/or father.

bundle: A collection of things wrapped together.

arguing: Expressing opinions in an angry way.

Comprehension Questions

1. What was the problem with the five brothers and sisters in the story?

2. What did Grandma give each sibling to break?

3. Could the siblings easily break the single sticks?

4. What did Grandma give them next, and could they break it?

5. What did the siblings learn from this experience?

Answers

1. They always fought with each other.

2. Grandma gave each sibling a single stick.

3. Yes, they could easily break the single sticks.

4. Grandma gave them a bundle of sticks tied together, and they couldn't break it.

5. They learned that when they stay together and support each other, they are stronger.

Expressions #8

Can I please get two tickets for Batman?

Sure, no problem.

Sorry, the 7:00 viewing is sold out. Would you like tickets for the 8:00 show?

That sounds great. Thank you.

I'd like a large popcorn and a large Coke, please.

Sure.

Would you like to add some candy and make it a combo?

Where would you like to sit?

I'd like to sit in the back (middle/front/aisle).

Do you have assigned seating?

No, you can sit anywhere you want.

Yes, where would you like to sit?

What size would you like?

A small (medium, large) please.

Anything else?

Sure, I'll have a medium coke.

No, that's it. Thank you.

Dialogue #1:

Tom: Hi, can I get four tickets for James Bond, please?

Jenny: Sure, the 7:30 viewing?

Tom: Yes, please. And do you have any combos that include popcorn and drinks?

Jenny: We do, but you don't buy them here. You can purchase them at the concession.

Tom: Okay, thank you.

Dialogue #2:

Tim: Can I see your ticket please?

Carrie: Here you go.

Tim: For the 8:00? You have to wait a few more minutes before going in.

Carrie: Oh really? Okay.

Phrasal Verbs #8: Booked Off

Kevin and Tony are talking about their plans.

Kevin*:* What are you doing for summer vacation?

Tony: Well, I just **booked off** some time to go camping. I need to **chill out.** I've been **burning the candle at both ends** for months now.

Kevin: I know. You **work like a dog**. Where are you **headed to**?

Tony: To Cultus Lake. It's beautiful there plus there are waterslides for the kids and a pub for me!

Kevin: That sounds just about perfect. I'm going to do a mini **staycation** and do lots of day hikes and stuff like that.

Tony: Sounds nice too. Where do you like hiking?

Kevin: I'm just **getting into it** now. I bought a book though so I'll do some stuff from there.

Vocabulary

booked off: Submitted a request for time off of work.

chill out: Relax; take a break.

burning the candle at both ends: Working many hours, long into the night.

work like a dog: Working too much to the point of exhaustion.

headed to: Going.

staycation: A vacation where you just stay home.

getting into it: Starting something.

Practice

1. I'm not sure about tennis yet. I'm just _____.

2. You can't keep _____.

3. Where are you _____ for vacation?

4. I don't want to spend a lot of money. What about a _____?

5. I've _____ the first two weeks of August.

6. I _____ but what do I have to show for it?

7. I plan to just _____ at home this weekend.

Answers

1. getting into it

2. burning the candle at both ends

3. headed to

4. staycation

5. booked off

6. work like a dog

7. chill out

Time Expressions #8: At One Time

Patty and Ryan are talking about being a police officer.

Patty: So what did you want to be **when you were growing up**?

Ryan: Oh, **at one time**, I wanted to be a police officer but I see now that working the **night shift** is terrible for your health.

Patty: Not only that, but I think that cops are **constantly** changing between nights and **days**.

Ryan: My friend told me that they change shifts **weekly** and that he sometimes **loses track of days**.

Patty: For sure, you'd **never** get a good night's sleep. But, maybe you'd be so exhausted that you could fall asleep **in no time**. I would never want to do it though!

Vocabulary

when you were growing up: The time period from birth to approximately 18 years old.

at one time: A specific point of time in the past.

night shift: Working during the night.

constantly: Always

days: In this case, it refers to working days instead of nights, for certain jobs where people regularly work at night (nurse, factory worker, doctor, police officer, etc.).

weekly: Something that happens each week.

loses track of days: Can't remember what day of the week it is, usually due to being very tired or traveling across time zones.

never: Describes something that doesn't happen.

in no time: In a short amount of time.

Practice

1. You'll be done _____ if you concentrate.

2. I'm lucky—I work all _____ next month.

3. _____, I considered joining the military.

4. That guy always _____ because he travels so much.

5. I _____ have to tell my kids to clean up their dishes.

6. _____, did you get to eat a lot of junk food?

7. I _____ smoke.

8. I know it's weird, but I prefer the _____.

9. I have to get a _____ injection for two months.

Answers

1. in no time

2. days

3. at one time

4. loses track of days

5. constantly

6. when you were growing up

7. never

8. night shift

9. weekly

Vocabulary #9

Online dating
Meaning: Finding a love match through the Internet.

Examples:

Have you ever tried *online dating*?

I met my wife through *online dating*.

What's your favourite app for *online dating*?

Online shopping
Meaning: Buying things using the Internet.

Examples:

I prefer *online shopping* to going to stores.

I hate *online shopping*, especially for clothes and shoes. I like to try things on first.

There are some big advantages to *online shopping,* especially for comparing prices.

Out of shape
Meaning: Not in good health from bad diet or lack of exercise.
Examples:

I'm so *out of shape*. I get tired walking up the stairs.

I hate being *out of shape* but it's hard to exercise since I broke my leg.

My trainer told me that I'm not *out of shape*. I don't believe her though.

Parking
Meaning: A place to put a car when you're not driving it.
Examples:

Parking is so expensive in Toronto. Let's take the subway.

Help me look for *parking*, okay? It's busy around here.

There must be some free *parking*. Let's keep looking.

Part-time job
Meaning: A job that is less than 40 hours per week.

Examples:

I had a *part-time job* at Burger King when I was in high school.

I need more money! I'm looking for a *part-time job*.

Did you have a *part-time job* when you were a student?

Pick up
Meaning: Get.

Examples:

I have to *pick up* Tom from soccer tonight at 6:30.

Let's *pick up* a pizza for dinner tonight.

Do you want to *pick up* some groceries on your way home from work?

Police
Meaning: A group of people who enforce laws/maintain order in a society.

Examples:

Should we call the *police*?

There's a *police* station down the street from my house.

There were lots of *police* at the protest yesterday.

Problem
Meaning: Negative situation or thing.

Examples:

 My *problem* is that I hate studying!

What's the *problem*?

Keith always has so many *problems*.

Practice

online dating, problem, online shopping, police, out of shape, parking, part-time job, pick up

1. Can I help you? What's the _____?

2. What kind of _____ are you looking for?

3. I'm so _____. Please slow down.

4. Let's _____ a pizza for dinner.

5. I prefer _____ to stores for most things.

6. Have you ever tried _____?

7. There's a _____ station near my house.

8. Help me look for _____.

Answers

1. problem

2. part-time job

3. out of shape

4. pick up

5. online shopping

6. online dating

7. police

8. parking

Dialogue #9: Watching a Baseball Game

John and Mel are chatting during a baseball game.

John: Did you see that hit?

Mel: Wait. What happened? I was checking my emails!

John: They might show it on the screen again. Alex Garcia took a super low pitch and popped it right over the head of the second baseman.

Mel: Ahhh. I always miss the action.

John: Well, put your phone away my friend! Haha.

Mel: You're right. It's a terrible habit.

Check Your Understanding

1. Why didn't Mel see the hit?

2. What is Mel's terrible habit?

3. Who hit the ball?

Answers

1. He didn't see it because he was checking his emails.

2. His terrible habit is that he's always on his phone.

3. Alex Garcia hit the ball.

Story #9: The Frog and the Ox

Once upon a time in a happy meadow, there was a small frog named Freddy. He liked to **hop** around and enjoy life. One day, he saw a **massive, mighty** ox named Oliver and wished he could be as impressive.

Freddy told Oliver about his wish, and the ox decided to teach him a lesson. Oliver puffed up his chest to look even bigger, but it didn't work, and he made a funny "POP!" sound. Freddy giggled and said, "Oliver, it seems trying to be something you're not doesn't work."

Oliver agreed and told Freddy, "Be happy with who you are. True greatness comes from being yourself." After that, Freddy learned to appreciate his small size and the things that made him special. He hopped around the **meadow**, spreading joy and wisdom to everyone he met. And so, in the happy meadow, Freddy lived contentedly ever after.

The Moral

The moral of this fable is: "Be happy with who you are and appreciate your own unique qualities. Trying to be someone you're not might not bring the happiness you seek."

Vocabulary

hop: Jump.

mighty: Very large or strong.

massive: Huge.

Comprehension Questions

1. Why did Freddy, the little frog, approach Oliver, the mighty ox?

2. What did Oliver, the wise ox, do to try to teach Freddy a lesson?

3. What happened when Oliver tried to make himself even larger?

4. What did Freddy learn from the experience with Oliver?

5. What did Freddy realize about true greatness through his encounter with Oliver?

Answers

1. Freddy admired the ox's size and strength.

2. Oliver inflated his chest, making himself even larger than usual, in an attempt to show Freddy the challenges that come with trying to be something you're not.

3. When Oliver inflated his chest, he let out a loud "POP!"

4. Freddy learned to appreciate his own unique qualities instead of wishing to be someone else.

5. Freddy realized that greatness comes from being oneself, and it's not necessarily linked to size or outward appearances.

Expressions #9

Do you have your library card?

Yes, just a second.

How many books can I take out?

You can take out 10 books at a time.

When are they due?

They are due in two weeks.

Is there a quiet study space?

Yes, it's in the room at the back.

Where's the bathroom?

It's downstairs, on your left.

You have a late fine of $1.70. Would you like to pay for that now?

Yes, I can.

I lost my library card. Can I get a new one?

Sure, no problem.

Yes, but there's a $10 fee.

Dialogue #1:

Tom: Hi, it's my first time here. I just have a few questions.

Jenny: Sure, how can I help?

Tom: How many books can I take out at a time?

Jenny: You can take out up to 20 books.

Tom: And how long can I keep them?

111

Jenny: 3 weeks for books and 2 weeks for movies and music.

Tom: Finally, do you have a quiet study space?

Jenny: Unfortunately not but it's usually pretty quiet between 10 and 2.

Tom: Great, thanks for your help.

Dialogue #2:

Tim: I can't check these books out for some reason.

Carrie: Hmmm...let me take a look.

Tim: Oh, it says that you have overdue fees of $22 on your account. You can't take out more books if it's over $20.

Carrie: Really? I'll pay the fine now then.

Tim: Sure.

Phrasal Verbs #9: Worn Out

Sarah: Hey Lucy, how was your day?

Lucy: Ohhh...I'm **beat up** and **worn out**! I had to **run around** all over town and then I was the last one at the office so I had to **lock up**. It took me so long to **get out of** there.

Sarah: That sounds terrible. Are you going to **turn in** early?

Lucy: Yeah. I'm going to **wash up** and **head towards** bed. Goodnight.

Vocabulary

beat up: Weary; tired.

worn out: Tired.

run around: Do lots of things in a short amount of time.

lock up: Secure something.

get out of: Leave; avoid something.

turn in: Go to bed.

wash up: Clean (dishes or body).

head towards: Go to.

Practice

1. I'm _____ from that soccer game. You don't look _____ though! How is that possible?

2. Can you _____ the dishes please?

3. Can you _____ at close? I need to leave a bit early tonight so I can't do it.

4. I know you want to _____ this but there's no way to avoid it.

5. Let's _____ home. I'm starting to get tired and hungry!

6. Why don't you _____ and have an early night?

7. I have to _____ after I drop the kids off at school and do a million things.

Answers

1. worn out/beat up

2. wash up

3. lock up

4. get out of

5. head towards

6. turn in

7. run around

Time Expressions #9: In the 40s

Harry is talking to his grandmother about the past.

Harry: So what was life like **in the past**?

Dianne: Well, I grow up **in the 40s**. It was an interesting time. World War 2 has just ended and the economy was booming as all the men returned home. It was the defining moment of the **20th century** in my opinion.

Harry: Oh wow. That does sound like an interesting time. I personally can't imagine life without the Internet.

Dianne: I know it seems crazy now, right? You kids born in the **21st century** have just grown up with it. I wonder what life will be like **in 20 years' time**?

Harry: That's **way off in the future**. Who knows! Maybe flying cars?

Dianne: We'll see if I live **long enough** to see it!

Vocabulary

in the past: A point before the time being mentioned.

in the 40s: 1940-1949.

20th century: 1900-1999.

21st century: 2000-2099.

in 20 years' time: 20 years into the future. For example, if it's 2020 now, then 2040.

way off in the future: Many years later.

long enough: A period of time that is adequate.

Vocabulary

1. It's been _____. He should be done by now.

2. _____, I used to drink a lot but I've cut back now.

3. The Internet was invented during the _____.

4. Oh, that's _____. I haven't even thought about it yet.

5. I was born _____.

6. In the _____, kids don't know what life was like before the Internet.

7. I hope to be retired _____.

Answers

1. long enough

2. in the past

3. 20th century

4. way off in the future

5. in the 40s

6. 21st century

7. in 20 years' time

Vocabulary #10

Rush hour
Meaning: The busiest times to drive, usually in the morning and after work.

Examples:

Rush hour traffic is terrible in Vancouver.

I hate coming home from work during *rush hour*.

I avoid driving during *rush hour*.

Save money
Meaning: Have more money in the bank by not wasting money on unnecessary things.

Examples:

We need to *save money*. I hate using credit cards all the time.

It's difficult to *save money* in Vancouver.

We can *save money* by cancelling Netflix.

Scattered showers
Meaning: Rain that is on and off.

Examples:

There will be *scattered showers* tomorrow. Let's see how it looks in the morning.

The weather forecast is showing *scattered showers* this weekend.

There will be *scattered showers*, starting tonight and lasting for a couple of days.

School night
Meaning: The night before you have to go to school (usually Sunday—Thursday).

Examples:

Jimmy! It's a *school night*. Go to bed now.

Isn't it a *school night*? Why are asking me to have a sleepover?

On *school nights*, I try to have the kids in bed by 8:00.

Seniors

Meaning: Older people (usually 65+).

Examples:

Are there a lot of *seniors* in your city?

Is there a *seniors'* centre in your town?

The best thing about being a *senior* is that you get lots of discounts.

Shades

Meaning: Sunglasses.

Examples:

Have you seen my *shades*?

Just a minute. I need to grab my *shades* before we leave.

I want to buy some new *shades*. I'm not sure if I should spend hundreds of dollars on a pair.

Shop around

Meaning: Compare prices.

Examples:

Did you *shop around*? I'm sure you could find it cheaper.

I like to *shop around* for things that cost more than $100.

I'm too lazy to *shop around*! I just buy the first thing that looks like a good deal.

Sidewalk

Meaning: A raised area next to a road where people can walk.

Examples:

Walk on the *sidewalk,* please!

I wish there were more *sidewalks* in my city.

You should ride your bike on the road, not the *sidewalk*.

Practice

rush hour, save money, scattered showers, school night, seniors, shades, shop around, sidewalk

1. Let's _____ for a new car. We can find a better deal.

2. The weather forecast says _____.

3. What's your secret for _____? I'm terrible at it!

4. I hate driving during _____.

5. _____ was my favourite subject at school.

6. No, you can't hang out with Tim. It's a _____.

7. I hate it when bicycles go on the _____.

Answers

1. shop around

2. scattered showers

3. saving money

4. rush hour

5. science

6. school night

7. sidewalk

Dialogue #10: Running Late

Zeke wants to let Sid know that he is running late.

Zeke: Sid. Hi. So sorry but I'm going to be late for dinner.

Sid: Oh, okay. What time do you think you'll get here?

Zeke: By 7:00 at the latest, I think. There was an accident ahead of me on the highway.

Sid: Oh no! Is it cleared?

Zeke: It will be soon I think. It looks like the police are finishing up now and traffic is moving slowly.

Sid: Sure. See you when you get here. No rush. I'll just have a glass of wine and wait.

Zeke: Thanks for understanding. I appreciate it.

Check Your Understanding

1. What time was their dinner plan?

2. Who is going to be late?

3. What will Sid do while he waits?

Answers

1. Their dinner meeting time was before 7:00.

2. Zeke is going to be late.

3. He's going to have a glass of wine.

Story #10: The Ant and the Grasshopper

In a meadow, ant Andy worked hard, **storing** food for winter, while grasshopper Greg enjoyed **carefree** days. As winter approached, Andy was well-prepared, but Greg, unready, asked for food. Andy, disappointed, reminded Greg of the warnings.

Realizing his mistake, Greg felt regret. Winter came, and Andy **thrived**, while Greg struggled. The story teaches us that preparation and hard work lead to success, emphasizing responsibility and planning.

The Moral

The moral of the story is: "It's important to work hard and plan for the future so that you can be prepared for tough times."

Vocabulary

storing: Keeping for future use.

carefree: Without worry.

thrived: Did well.

Comprehension Questions

1. Who were the two friends in the story?

2. What did Andy do to prepare for winter?

3. How did Greg spend his time while Andy was preparing for winter?

4. When winter arrived, how did Andy and Greg do?

5. What is the moral of the story?

Answers

1. The two friends in the story were Andy ant and Greg the grasshopper.

2. Andy worked hard, storing food for winter, and reinforcing his anthill.

3. Greg spent his time playing, singing, and dancing.

4. Andy thrived in winter because he had stored enough food and made preparations. Greg struggled because he hadn't planned for the cold season.

5. The moral of the story is that it's important to work hard and plan for the future.

Expressions #10

Hi, what can I get you?

I'd like a medium drip coffee.

What size would you like?

A medium, (small, large, extra-large) please.

Would you like room?

Yes, please. (Room for cream or milk at the top).

Where can I find cream?

It's over there, by the door.

What time do you close?

We close at 9:00.

Do you have any food?

Yes, we have paninis and cookies.

No, sorry we don't.

Do you need anything else?

No thanks. That's it I think.

Do you have a points card?

No, I don't. Can I get one?

Yes, let me get it.

Dialogue #1:

123

Tom: Hi, what can I get you?

Jenny: I'd like a mint-chocolate chip Frappuccino, please.

Tom: Sure, what size would you like?

Jenny: Medium please. To go.

Tom: Sure.

Dialogue #2:

Tim: Hi, what would you like?

Carrie: What do you recommend? I don't really like coffee that much.

Tim: Do you want a hot or cold drink?

Carrie: Hot, please.

Tim: Sure, we have some nice teas or hot chocolate.

Carrie: Okay, I'll have a large hot chocolate then. For here.

Phrasal Verbs #10: Cross Off

Mary: Uggghhhh...I have so many things on my to-do list! I have to **drop off** my dry cleaning, **fill up** the car, and **knock out** a ton of cleaning.

Molly: Oh no! Why don't you let me **help out** with some of that stuff? I honestly have nothing to do this afternoon. We can get some of that stuff **crossed off** your list.

Mary: You want to **give up** your free time to help me out? That's amazing!

Molly: Sure. No problem.

Mary: Maybe you can **move in** too? I always have too many things to do!

Vocabulary

drop off: Leave something somewhere.

fill up: Add something, to the fullest point.

knock out: Do things.

help out: Offer assistance.

crossed off: Using a pen to strike through something on a list or document.

give up: Stop trying.

move in: The act of changing where you live.

Practice

1. Can you _____ Tim at school on your way to work?

2. Why don't we _____ Mary by shovelling her driveway?

3. I know that you want to _____ but it'll be worth it in the end.

4. Let's _____ this cleaning and then we can enjoy the rest of the weekend.

5. It's _____. I think Tony did it already.

6. Oh no! The light just came on. Let's find a gas station to _____ at.

7. I can't hang out this weekend. I have to _____ to my new place.

Answers

1. drop off

2. help out

3. give up

4. knock out

5. crossed off

6. fill up

7. move in

Time Expressions #10: Race Against Time

Sara and Lucy are talking about a deadline they have to meet at work.

Sara: Does it feel like we're in a **race against time** with this project? When is the **deadline** again?

Lucy: Oh yeah, we're **behind the eight ball** for sure. It was **yesterday at 9 am.**

Sara: Oh shoot. This happens **every month**. Why do we always seem to start this stuff **the day before**? We should have started it **on Monday.**

Lucy: I know. I agree completely but it's out of our hands. Jen is the one who assigns this stuff and she's so disorganized.

Sara: I wonder what other companies must think of us?

Vocabulary

race against time: Trying to finish something before the time is up.

deadline: When something should be finished.

behind the eight ball: Late finishing something.

yesterday at 9 am: The previous day at 9:00 in the morning.

every month: Describes something that happens each month.

the day before: One day prior to the time being mentioned. For example, if the deadline is Tuesday, the day before is Monday.

Practice

1. I always feel so nervous _____ a test.

2. It's honestly a _____ here. We need to hurry up.

3. He's usually _____ when it comes to his taxes.

4. The meeting was _____. Why weren't you there?

5. The _____ for this is Tuesday at 5:00.

6. It's the same thing _____ for this guy.

Answers

1. the day before

2. race against time

3. behind the eight ball

4. yesterday at 9 am

5. deadline

6. every month

Before You Go

If you found this book useful, please leave a review wherever you bought it. It will help other English learners, like yourself find this resource.

Join my email list for English learners here: www.eslspeaking.org/learn-english. You'll get tips, resources, and lessons, delivered straight to your inbox.

You can find me here:

Pinterest: www.pinterest.com/eslspeaking

YouTube: www.youtube.com/@JackieBolen

Email: jb.business.online@gmail.com

Made in the USA
Columbia, SC
01 February 2025

ba8c4254-4ffe-4b1a-a26e-0a72019490ecR01